THE OPEN MEDIA PAMPHLET SERIES

OTHER OPEN MEDIA PAMPHLET SERIES TITLES

CORPORATE MEDIA AND THE THREAT TO DEMOCRACY
Robert W. McChesney
80 pages / $5.95 / ISBN: 1-888363-47-9

MEDIA CONTROL: THE SPECTACULAR ACHIEVEMENTS
OF PROPAGANDA Noam Chomsky
64 pages / $5.95 / ISBN: 1-888363-49-5

GENE WARS: THE POLITICS OF BIOTECHNOLOGY
Kristin Dawkins
64 pages / $4.95 / ISBN: 1-888363-48-7

GLOBALIZING CIVIL SOCIETY: RECLAIMING OUR RIGHT
TO POWER David C. Korten
80 pages / $5.95 / ISBN: 1-888363-59-2

ZAPATISTA ENCUENTRO: DOCUMENTS FROM THE
1996 ENCOUNTER FOR HUMANITY AND AGAINST NEOLIBERALISM
The Zapatistas
64 pages / $5.95 / ISBN: 1-888363-58-4

PROPAGANDA, INC.: SELLING AMERICA'S CULTURE
TO THE WORLD Nancy Snow
80 pages / $5.95 / ISBN: 1-888363-74-6

A SUSTAINABLE ECONOMY FOR THE 21ST CENTURY
Juliet Schor
64 pages / $5.95 / ISBN: 1-888363-75-4

THE UMBRELLA OF U.S. POWER
Noam Chomsky
80 pages / $5.95 / 1-888363-85-1

THE CASE AGAINST LAMEDUCK IMPEACHMENT
Bruce Ackerman
80 pages / $8.00 / ISBN: 1-58322-004-6

ACTS OF AGGRESSION: POLICING "ROGUE STATES"
Noam Chomsky, Edward W. Said, Ramsey Clark
64 pages / $6.95 / ISBN: 1-58322-005-4

THE PROGRESSIVE GUIDE TO
ALTERNATIVE MEDIA AND ACTIVISM
Project Censored
144 pages / $10.00 / ISBN: 1-888363-84-3

MICRORADIO AND DEMOCRACY
Greg Ruggiero
64 pages / $5.95 / ISBN: 1-58322-000-3

THE LAST ENERGY WAR: THE BATTLE OVER UTILITY DEREGULATION
Harvey Wasserman
80 pages / $5.95 / ISBN: 1-58322-017-8

TO ORDER ADDITIONAL SERIES TITLES CALL 1 (800) 596-7437

THE OPEN MEDIA PAMPHLET SERIES

Poems for the Nation

A Collection of Contemporary Political Poems

Edited by **ALLEN GINSBERG**
with Andy Clausen and Eliot Katz

OPEN MEDIA PAMPHLET SERIES EDITOR GREG RUGGIERO

SEVEN STORIES PRESS / New York

LIBRARY OF CONGRESS CATALOGING-IN-PUBLICATION DATA

Poems for the nation: a collection of contemporary political poems / edited
by Allen Ginsberg; with Andy Clausen and Eliot Katz.—A Seven Sto-
ries Press 1st ed.
     p.   cm. — (Open media pamphlet series; 15)
     ISBN 1-58322-012-7 (pbk.)
     1. Political poetry, American. 2. United States—Politics and gov-
ernment—20th century—Poetry. 3. American poetry—20th century. I.
Series. II. Ginsberg, Allen, 1926–1997. III. Katz, Eliot. IV. Clausen, Andy.
PS595.P634 P64 1999
811'.54080358 21—dc21   99-041330

Typesetting by Michael Cote and Mari Schneider Cote
9 8 7 6 5 4 3 2 1
Printed in the U.S.A.

Acknowledgments

Unless otherwise noted below, all copyrights for the poems and prose included in this volume are retained by the authors. All rights reserved.

Andy Clausen's "More Same Old" appeared in *40th Century Man* (Autonomedia, 1997). William Burroughs' "Remember Control" is printed with the permission of the William S. Burroughs Trust. Wanda Coleman's "Welfare Quean" was previously published in *Bathwater Wine* (Black Sparrow Press, Santa Rosa, CA) © 1998 by Wanda Coleman, reprinted here with the permission of the author. David Cope's "Sirens & flashing lights stop" appeared in *Silences for Love* (Humana Press, 1998). Jayne Cortez's "Cultural Operations" © 1999 by Jayne Cortez. Allen Ginsberg's "New Democracy Wish List" appeared in *Death & Fame* (HarperCollins, 1999) and is reprinted here by permission of the Allen Ginsberg Trust. Allen Ginsberg's "Television Address" will appear in the forthcoming *Deliberate Prose: Selected Essays 1952-1995* (HarperCollins, 2000). Aimée Grunberger's "Here in The Western World" is printed with permission of the Estate of Aimée Grunberger. Eliot Katz's "Dinosaur Love" appeared in *Unlocking the Exits* (Coffee House Press, 1999). Carl Rakosi's "Down to Earth Suite" appeared in *Earth Suite* (Etruscan Books, 1997), included here by permission of the author. Anne Waldman's "Born Again Blues" © 1999 Fast Speaking Music, used by permission of the author. An earlier version of Peter Lamborn Wilson's "The Sacred and Profane History of Money" appeared in the "Money" issue of *Whole Earth Review*.

All royalties from this volume are being donated to the following three activist groups that Allen Ginsberg supported:

Fairness and Accuracy in Reporting (FAIR)
130 W. 25th Street
New York, NY 10001
Phone: 212-633-6700
Fax: 212-727-7668
E-mail: fair@fair.org
Website: www.fair.org

PEN Freedom to Write Committee
568 Broadway
NewYork, NY 10012
Phone: 212-334-1660
Fax: 212-334-2181
E-mail: elham@pen.org, diana@pen.org
Website: www.pen.org

War Resisters League
339 Lafayette Street
New York, NY 10012
Phone: 212-228-0450
Fax: 212-228-6193
E-mail: wrl@igc.org
Website: www.nonviolence.org/wrl

Readers are encouraged to contact these groups for more information.

Contents

II. Allen Ginsberg as Poet-Activist

Introduction

During the last year and a half of his life, Allen Ginsberg phoned various poet friends to ask if they had written social verses opposing America's rightward drift or otherwise speaking their political minds. After discussing the need for an assemblage of current politically aware poetry with editors from *The Nation,* one of his favorite sources of political analysis and information, *The Nation* asked Allen to edit a small anthology for its pages. With a Congress dominated by the Gingrich-led Republican Right and a centrist president erasing many of the Democratic Party's liberal traditions, Allen felt a political poetry issue might help put fairness, compassion, and progressive political vision back into the national discussion. He also thought these verses would energize *The Nation's* poetry selections.

Although the project was incomplete at the time of his death in April 1997, Allen had spent much time collecting, selecting, and even editing poems. Those he wished to include were placed in a file folder marked "poems to use." For some poets, several pieces remained under consideration in the "poems to use" folder, from which Allen was going to pick one. At Bob Rosenthal's request, poets Andy Clausen and Eliot Katz made these selections—working with Allen's detailed notes, recalling personal conversations with Allen about this project (including an hours-long kitchen-table discussion between Allen and Andy paging through every submission received), and their own editorial judgment in a few cases where Allen's final preference wasn't clear. We all then discussed which other pieces could best fill out this volume (see Section II).

Several of the poems in this volume were revised by authors based on Allen's editing suggestions. According to Andy Clausen, "Allen was a great editor line for line, word for word. He could find the gem: he knew lining

1

and how it affected the reader's eyes; he knew meter and could excise the excessive music, scratching out articles and conjunctions; but most of all he could cut through his own personal prejudices and go to the meat, the text. His writing style and taste in poetry were as variegated and all-inclusive as I've ever known the definition of a human being to be."

If Allen had remained alive to complete this project, he may very well have continued asking writers he liked for additional work. While some of Allen's favorite contemporary poets are included, this book is not a collection of Allen's favorite poets or poems. It is a volume filled with poems that Allen wanted published because he believed they could help inspire an increased social consciousness for the new millennium. Besides the poems Allen had collected, this volume also includes tributes to Allen's historic importance as a poet-activist by longtime poet friends, Eileen Myles, Ed Sanders, and Amiri Baraka; a poem for Allen written by his brother, Eugene Brooks; a poem ("New Democracy Wish List") that Allen himself had written with political advice for then newly elected President Clinton; and a never-before-published speech Allen gave in 1972 which bubbles with his unique blend of political acumen and poetic verve and which remains relevant today.

While *The Nation,* after Allen's death, decided against publishing, we are thankful to the Open Media Pamphlet Series for printing the work Allen compiled. Allen admired Open Media's political contributions from their beginnings during the '91 Gulf War. In late 1996, he did a benefit reading for Open Media in his last performance at Columbia University, so it is fitting that this volume finds its home in the Pamphlet Series.

Through his groundbreaking, visionary poetry and his principled life, Allen Ginsberg provided inspiration to poets and activists throughout the world five decades. From his outspokenness against Eisenhower-era political and sexual repression to his protests against the Vietnam War, from his willingness to sit on Rocky Flats railroad tracks to stop plutonium manufacturing to his opposition to censorship and ecological destruction East & West, Allen always put his body and his poetry on the line. Much of his office's daily work was spent sending letters to public officials, making contacts between poets and political organizers, gathering information about social issues of Allen's concern, and making donations to activist groups whose work Allen felt important. (Royalties from this collection will be donated to 3 such groups. See Acknowlegments p. ii.) Allen was a prophetic poet exposing human injustice in the tradition of William Blake and extending Walt Whitman's democratic vision for America. In this volume, Amiri Baraka writes that Allen was "as well, a publicist, perhaps the best we knew of poetry itself." With this new collection, Allen continues his role as a promoter for poetry—and for its potential to inspire a more compassionate, democratic spirit & politics for the nation & planet.

Eliot Katz
Assistant Editor
Poems for the Nation

Bob Rosenthal
Trustee
Allen Ginsberg Trust

I. Poems for the Nation

Follow Orders

Drag the rainbow into the interrogation room.
Use thumbscrews on clouds if necessary.
Arrest the wind for being shiftless.
Take a lake to headquarters for loitering.
Sentence aspens to 30 years hard labor
    for having leaves that quiver.
Turn rainforests into deserts.
Put deserts behind bars because
    poets see a world in a grain of sand.
Accuse sanddunes of being drifters.
Accuse snowdrifts of being drifters.
Tell the birds to shut up and listen to your song.
Cross-examine snowflakes till they break into tears.
Accuse a leech of being a leech.
Accuse a sponge of being a sponge.
Accuse a yawn of being a yawn.
Search milkweed-pods as suspicious characters.
Hog-tie will-o-the-wisps,
    take them into custody.
Tar-and-feather every inch of living soil
    that refuses to be covered with asphalt.
Put Lake Michigan on the witness stand
    to testify against Lake Superior.
Arraign the rain, indict the kite
    and prosecute the bandicoot.
Charge lightning and thunder
    for practicing without a license.
Charge the view from the skyscraper
    with making people look like ants.
Warn autumn colors to stop rioting.
Throw the rich odor of thawing earth in a dungeon.
Frisk the shimmer of light on moonlit water.
Search crotches of virgin timber for concealing drugs.

Straitjacket elephants for jacking off with their nose.
Make a bear paw the Bible to take oath.
Ban the banana because
    it reminds you of something.
Flog alpenglow with a rubber hose
    under a hundred-watt lightbulb.
Slaughterhouse moonbeams.
Summon the lemon, subpoena the peanut,
    impeach the peach, arraign the terrain.
Order the space between the stars and
    the space between molecules to change place.
Order turtles to get license plates.
Order sunflowers to pay their electric bills
    or the sun be disconnected.
Order rats to join the rat race.
Order orifice and artifice to be reversed.
Order ripples of water, ripples of light,
    ripples of heat, ripples of shade
        to do your bidding.
Order poems to close down and move to Mexico
    where they can get words to work
        for one-fifth what they're paid here.
Millepedes must obey or be drawn-and-thousanded.
Decapitate ecstatic tomfoolery.
Give the finger to the wind
    for being fresh with you.
Gesticulate before the bristlecone pine
    how you made more money than anyone.
Brag to the Pleiades you played the stock market
    better than anyone.
Tell your Death you're going to hold your breath
    till it grants your wish.
Sentence leaf-shadows to the electric chair
    for seducing millions of youths.
Torture the Ocean till it talks,
    and none of this surf-sound mumbo-jumbo.
Reduce to toothpicks the oldest biggest trees.

Tame wildflowers and coat them with plastic
    and mount them on wire stems.
Buy the water, buy the earth, buy the sky.
Sell the water, sell the earth, sell the sky.
Beat up the night 'cause it's black.
Spit at the sun 'cause it's yellow.
Massacre the dawn it's red.
Chart how many ants you can kill.
Ambush waterfalls with machetes,
    mutilate them beyond recognition.
Assassinate the last condor in your spare time.
Assign hit-men to rub out hummingbirds
    while paring your nails.
Assign hit-men to rub out dolphins
    while paring your nails.
Step into your mile-long limousine
    snort a thousand dollars
        and tell the chauffeur—
    "Next Universe, please."

Barbara Barg

Temporary America
Dedicated to all temporary workers

First they bust the union
Then they bust my ass
In Temporary America
Don't want no organization
In the working class
In Temporary America

Contempt for the worker
Is what you get
In Temporary America
No job security
No benefits
In Temporary America

When frustration is high
People go insane
In Temporary America
Picking up guns
Blowing folks away
In Temporary America

It's not the tv
Makes violence thrive
It's Temporary America
I lay awake in my bed
As the bullets fly
Through Temporary America

The food is fast
And the work is dumb
In Temporary America

Workers praying
For Christ to come
To Temporary America

My rent is high
My ink is red
In Temporary America
I never seem
To come out ahead
In Temporary America

I'm so tired of living
In Temporary America
In temporary, contemporary
Contempt contempt contempt
For Temporary America

William Burroughs

Remember Control

Remember Control. Supposedly from the planet Venus, monitored by Willi Dieches and Brenda Dunks… Not surprising that an alien or discarnate intelligence would communicate thru a computer very much more advanced than any ouiji board. But their communication will be subject to the limitations of the computer, so if it sounds without emotion well that the instrument is without emotion does not mean the programmer is similarly handicapped.

"You gonna work me over?" says the young fag suspect enticingly unbuttoning his shirt, "you meaty blond beast…"

The meaty blond narc recoils in horror "Why you scum you."

The fag caresses his crotch, "Blond beast, I am here for your pleasure." With a bestial cry the narc hits the suspect in the mouth. The super comes in.

"Mistake?? 10th of September?? This is the 10th of July 1996."

He throws a disapproving look at the boy on the floor with bloody mouth. "I told you Felton, keep your hands off the suspects… it makes us look well…"

Boy on the floor does a pig act crawling on all fours "Oink Oink Oink."

"Any violation on that?"

"Not much. Traces of heroin in shirt pocket…"

"Get it out of here…"

Boy hands the narcs a broken bloody tooth on his way out.

The virus is everywhere, no use looking for an old style witch in Lawrence Kansas. The whole ecosystem from Junkies (heroin at 28 an ounce) to street pushers, stool pigeons making buys with serial numbered bills, agents coming after them, wholesalers, narc Coast Guard, people making lots of money, the real money made by banks the launderers of drug money. But it all depends on the addict...

A vast cancer that keeps replicating & eliminating any threat of legalization or intelligent consideration with the strident hysteria of the threatened parasite. Worst of all Congressmen trying to pass a law making it an offense to suggest *discussion* of Drug Policy.

"Any form of maintenance is immoral," Anslinger said. The La Guardia Report? "You've done a great disservice by making these facts available." Emotions roused from moderation to violent hate... Malaysia and Singapore Death Penalty...

How do you neutralize it? Same old lies, the media... Cures? Little research, some experiments in Spain with thorazine knockout sleep & opium antagonists, apomorphine, Chinese herbs, acupuncture...

Painless cure with effective treatment for those who want to stop is the answer. Cheap maintenance for those who cannot or will not stop because of long term addiction. Maintenance is indicated for the very people for whom doctors are now forbidden to prescribe, those with a painful chronic illness.

"... Dr. Paul Goddard said that about 150,000 cancer patients had severe pain that was not relieved even by morphine and that an additional 700,000 people had intractable pain from conditions like shingles, a viral infection of the nerves." (*N.Y. Times*, pg B9 August 6, 1996)

Yank the one essential factor, money, and the whole system will collapse like a house of cards. It didn't exist before Harrison Narcotics act, 1914. No criminal addicts, no money laundering. There was no money in it. It was a minor health problem.

August 6, 1996

Andy Clausen

MORE SAME OLD

Why order us do what you can't & won't do
    for yourselves?
Why make us eat excrement to eat food?
Why make us breathe poison in order to secure shelter?

from the Adirondacks to the Gulf of Mexico
from Detroit's broken promise to someone else's
    private Idaho
from Fort Apache to where children denizen skid row
Where is there somewhere left for us to go?

Why talk to us like we're spit?
Why never satisfied with what we give?
Why demand we labor to destroy all we've learned?
To kowtow & grovel to get a fraction of what
    we've already earned?

Used to say it's a free country?
New motto is no new taxes
More interested in *anything* than us
Making money from Tehran to Texas
Promoting more barriers twixt the sexes
change worlds words health & welfare with
    lightening faxes
I think you'd kill Indians again just for a cut in taxes

from coast of Maine to the Gulf of Mexico
from Detroit's broken promise to Christian Identity's
    private Idaho
from Bed Stuy to where children denizen skid row
Is there somewhere left for us to go?

WELFARE QUEAN

red-faced you follow the loony white line to
the blue door where the 7 a.m. wait runs fifty deep

you in your unwashed crown your snaggled teeth
your aircraft-carrier hips you're snotting all
over America this bad gin morning fizzle you've just
run out of tissues so you use the flap of your grimy
muumuu worn fax paper thin the truth you've tried
to peddle did not feed or free you but has trapped
you in the dungeon of working ass poor doings

you fill out white forms in blue ink
twixt curses and prayers, check the red boxes

the helpers you consult are underpaid automatons who
smell of bureaucratic bugkill yet sniff down
their noses at you maurauder your larcenous fingers
filching their taxes you tinsel thugsta robbing
them of phone time with sweethearts you pernicious
promiscuous sloven spreading VD, AIDS and black
     males

of course you're allergic to work, would rather

     sleep till noon
     watch the soaps the blabfests the shitcoms
          (low self steam)
     stand on street corners swiggin' grape
          or sippin' coonshine
     loudtalkin' gamblin' prostitutin'

blue-brained under the white
sheets, gasping to the throb warning code red

a cliché with a skin condition as

seen by those spaced-out heads/those probing
amber eyes narrowed to amused slits denying your
claim on the dream o purple mountains of prose
charting your failures as you nut up under the
thunder of blows your majesty that kinkknot on your
psyche of course you're guilty of breaking illusion and
taking up too much sun of course you're guilty of
looting the nation's coffers of course you're lucky

to have
survived past thirty five—you

bloodwart on the schnoz of Christ

Jack Collom

To the tune of "Amazing Grace"

Appointed soil / sole ground of life
Slow growth since coastal dawn
    So recently your stuff was rife
    And soon O nearly gone

———

Eight hundred kinds / of birds delight
The North American air
    But forests're felled in a money-fight
    There'll be no nesting there

———

The western bluebird / sang among
The February sage
    Its warbles sweet were roundly flung
    Howe'er the snow did rage

———

A little liquid / trickles down
The thinness of the Platte
    A million burghers swell the town
    And that's the end of that

David Cope

Sirens & flashing lights stop

traffic where the strikers tried
to stop trucks plowing thru
their human wall
          & cops waded into
the jobless lines
collaring shouting men & women,
    tossing them into the wagons
& slamming the doors:
         high noon
    in the shadowless summer,
unseen eyes
peering thru the mirrored windows
        where others, jobless
for years or scrambling
as burger clerks, errand boys,
    part-timers & sweepers
to pay the rising
    rent & fill the hungry mouths,
succumb to
the scab siren's song of money.

Jayne Cortez

CULTURAL OPERATIONS

operation same old right-wing multinational
think-tank manipulation of history
geography and information
operation out-of-shape generals
still talking war & licking
plates in the cafeteria
operation desert dumbness
operation army for hire
operation thieves
still giving music awards
and patting each other on the back
for stealing and imitating and appropriating
operation what does it matter
as long as the mob gets theirs
& the queen gets hers
& the X slaves continue to pay tribute
& the colonies continue to pay rent
& the International Monetary Fund &
World Bank stay intact
& there are no mass unruly defaultations
& no reorganizational plans of advancement on
front burner of an urban rebellion
& as long as we act as silly and mediocre
and corrupt and greedy and repressed
as we're programmed to act
and don't explode
& globalize that explosion into
a redistribution of all there is to redistribute
then everything remains what it is
        operation deforestation
operation deprivation   operation privatization
operation falsification   operation contamination

operation marginalization   operation militarization
operation polarization   operation subordination
operation toxification   operation destabilization
operation termination   operation operation

Diane di Prima

GOOD CLEAN FUN

It's terrorism, isn't it, when you're afraid to answer the
    door for lack of a Green Card
afraid to look for work, walk into the hospital when yr
    child is sick,

and what else than terrorism cd you call those smallpox
    blankets we gave the Indians
the trail of tears, the raids on Ghost Dancing tribes
It's terrorism when you're forbidden to speak yr language
paddled for it, made to run a hundred laps in the snow
in your thin & holey sneakers. What do you call it
when you're locked in yr high school classroom, armed
    policemen
manning the halls? Isn't it terrorism to force a young
    woman
to talk to her parents abt her clandestine love
the child she will or will not carry? Is it terrorism
to shoot striking onion workers (1934), pick off AIM
    members one by one?

What happened to the Hampton family in Chicago—
    Fred Hampton blown away in his bed—
would you call that terrorism? Or the MOVE kids in
    Philadelphia
bombed in their home. Or all the stories we don't know
buried in throats stuffed w/ socks, or pierced w/ bullets.
Wd you call it terrorism, what happened at Wounded
    Knee
or the Drug Wars picking off
the youth of our cities— as they already picked off
twenty years ago— or terrified into silence— the ones
    who shd be leading us now—

you know the names.
What was COINTELPRO if not terrorism? What new
    initials are they calling it today?

Is Leonard Peltier a victim of terrorism?
Is Mumia Abu-Jamal?

Is it terrorism if you are terrified
of the INS, the IRS, the landlord, yr boss, the man
who might do yr job for less?
if you're scared of yr health insurance
no health insurance
scared of yr street, yr hallway, scared every month
you might not get to the 1st and the next measly check?

Is it terrorism to take food from hungry school-kids?
To threaten teenagers who still have hope enough
have joy enough to bring babies into this mess?

How has terrorism touched *you* shaped *your* life?
Are you afraid to go out, to walk in yr city, yr suburb, yr
    countryside?
To read, to speak yr own language, wear yr tribe's
    clothes?
Afraid of the thin-shelled birds w/ twisted necks
poisoned by nitrates, by selenium?
Afraid that the dawn will be silent, the forests grey?
Is it terrorism to fill the Dnieper w/ radiation?
or heat the ionosphere w/ magnetism "to see what will
    happen"?
    A wonderful weapon, they say, it will perturb
    the weather pattern, disrupt communications
Who are the terrorists in the lumber wars?
(the water wars are coming)
And we haven't even talked about AIDS and cancer.

IS THE ASSAULT ON NATIVE INTELLIGENCE &
    GOOD WILL

THAT WE CALL THE EVENING NEWS
ANYTHING OTHER THAN AN ACT OF TERROR?

What was the Gulf War but terrorism
wearing the death mask of order?— one big car bomb it
    was
the guys who drove it dying now
one by one— ignored

Is acid rain a form of terrorism? (Think for yourself.)
Is GATT or NAFTA anything but a pact among
    brigands— the World Bank, the IMF their back-up
    men?
How long before they fight over the spoils? Who'll do
    their fighting for them?

Is Alan Greenspan perhaps the biggest *known* & *named*
of our terrorist leaders, *here*, nurtured *here*,
trained *here*

the dark design of whose hearts makes
Hutu & Tutsi
Croat & Muslim & Serb
mere diversionary tactics before the onslaught

Eric Drooker

The Ballad of Loisaida

East Side girls they got no combs,
Keep away, keep away!
They shave their heads down to the bone,
We are from Loisaida!

Chorus:
    Keep away, you bully, bully boys!
    Keep away, keep away!
    Keep away, and don't you make a noise,
    We are from Loisaida!

East Side boys don't watch TV
They get their kicks on Avenue B
East Side girls they got no mops
They scrub the floor with riot cops

(Chorus)

East Side boys don't play guitars
They bang their music on metal bars
East Side girls they ain't for sale
They pierce their tongues with six inch nails

(Chorus)

East Side boys don't wear no suits
They stomp around in combat boots
East Side girls don't wear brassieres
They cover their breasts with stray cat ears

(Chorus)

East Side boys they got no lease
They get beaten up by riot police
East Side girls they just don't care
They dance all night in Tompkins Square

(Chorus)

East Side punks ain't got no fear
'Cause all them cops are drunk on beer
East Side cops work for the banks
They cruise around in armored tanks

(Chorus)

East Side kids they got no trees
They climb the fence on Avenue D
East Side wind doesn't make us cold
We hug our bodies 'till we grow old

(Chorus)

O East Side boys they got no cars. Keep a-way, keep a-way! They get a-round but nev-er get far, We are from Lo - is - ai - da! Keep a-way, you bul - ly, bul - ly boys! Keep a-way, keep a-way! Keep away and don't you make a noise, We are from Lo - is - ai - da!

Cliff Fyman

Vice, Advice & Eccentricities:
Life Growing Up in a Small Town
of A Hundred Fires, Cuba as told by
Luis Comabella in the Tenth Street Lounge

I was always hanging around
with the most depraved well-known
homosexuals in my little town
I was always most attracted
to the company of eccentrics
rather than the company of
humdrum bourgeois
I didn't like baseball
and that's very dangerous for a boy
in Cuba not to like
On the other hand
I was Cuban national champion
in the 100-meter butterfly
a style that pre-told
my later existence
I slept with the entire swim
team except one but that's
because I didn't want to sleep with him
I always considered the best
poem would be the lived
poem not the written poem
so I set out to live my life
in a poem
I was always influenced by Walt
Whitman
There were moments of ecstacy
moments of madness
actually a whole life of madness

Just before I left Cuba
at age 15 my father told
me three things
If I ever get syphilis
don't be ashamed to go
to a doctor   The second one
I forget   The third one was if
I ever find out you're gay
I'll put a bullet in your head
That's around the time
I left Cuba

Aimée Grunberger

Here In The Western World

We're off the beaten path,
and no poachers have even hoped
to trespass for several generations.
Eighty world governments
sleep like babies
knowing their gold is in the Fed.

We held our last war on
your old stomping grounds.
A very damp and uncomfortable
occupancy, but that's all history now.

Our planes splintered in your skies,
then sprinkled their metal skins
and their servicemen all over
your countryside and towns.

We eat dinner in full profile
before huge picture windows.
The neighbors pass by, walk dogs,
push strollers. No need to duck.
They wouldn't think of opening fire.

I read somewhere about a night
during the blitz when there were
fifteen hundred separate fires
in the city of London. At 2 a.m.,
from the Isle of Dogs to Kensington
the hoses ran dry all at once.
I have trouble getting my mind around that.

Sure, our New York is boarded up
and even leveled in places.
But that's different.
We accomplished that ourselves.
It was our own idea.

Nanao Sakaki

Let's Eat Stars

Believe me, children!

God made
Sky for airplanes
Coral reefs for tourists
Farms for agrichemicals
Rivers for dams
Forests for golf courses
Mountains for ski resorts
Wild animals for zoos
Trucks and cars for traffic tragedies
Nuclear power plants for ghost dance.

Don't worry, children!
The well never dries up.

Look at the evening glow!
Sunflowers in the garden.
Red dragonflies in the air.

A small child starts singing:

"Let's eat stars!"
        "Let's eat stars!"

Lawrence Ferlinghetti

From Work-in-Progress

'History is made
 of the lies of the victors'
  but you would never dream it
   from the covers of the textbooks
    nor from the way the victors are portrayed
     as super-benevolent altruists
      and lovers of the poor and downtrodden
       who never had a chance to
        rise up and write their own dubious stories
        in the mystery we call history
        (a running sea
         in which fish change color
          when cast upon the beach)
And the feelthy rich
 get filthier or richer or whatever
  because money really doesn't 'trickle down'
   but rises like anything hot
And they keep getting more medals
 for bad behavior and for agreeing that Yes
  Justice has been done and
   the stock market is open to everyone Long live usura
    and the status quo is the best ever
     for preserving the status quota
And in fact why not have historians who
        leave blanks in their writings
         to be filled in variously
          depending on who's in power
And anyway history isn't really history
until it's rewritten
or at least until
it repeats itself
And a lot of genocides and massacres
maybe never really happened

so the record should be corrected
like the Holocaust or the rape of Cuba and Nicaragua
    or Cambodia or Timor or the Ottoman Empire 1915
Even though even God can't change
a historical fact
(something that's actually happened
like a rape or a kiss)
And all those natives
in all those Third and Fourth World ghettos
  really always wanted to be conquered by Columbus
    the Great White Hope
And on and on into the sunset
  go the histories about how
    God was always on our side anyway
      and who is more fit to write the story than
        the victors themselves who are the fittest
          having survived and arrived at the summit
            of humanity's blind history
              where the prizes are awarded to the fittest
And anyway everyone except Plato knows that
    Truth Beauty Goodness are all relative
      especially Truth as she is extolled
        in the history books Amen *oh brother*
                              can you spare a dime?

Eliot Katz

Dinosaur Love

On the Museum of Natural History's 4th floor
I greeted my old friend:
"Hey, T. Rex! Long time, no see!"
My buddy flashed his killer teeth:
"Over two years, E. Katz,
I missed you."

Surprised, I asked, "You missed me?
I didn't know dinosaurs had emotions.
Rexy, did you know love?"

Rexy sighed: "I knew love
    not as humans can
but as humans do:
    love of self
    and love of finding something weaker
        to pounce upon.
E.Katz, can your species be saved
    by love's possibilities?"

"Rexy," I answered, "you haven't lost
your ability
to ask the tough question.
Let me ask you something we humans
have been curious about for centuries.
How did you die?"

"I don't know.
One day I looked around
and I wasn't there."

Tuli Kupferberg

PAINT IT RED (& BLACK)

*Tune: "Paint It Black" (Rolling Stones) with spoken
extensions. NOTE: Red & Black are the Anarchist colors.*

I see The White House & I
    want to paint it Red
Rabbi Jesus whispers to me:
    "Besser Red zan Dead."
I see The Kremlin & I'm
    gonna paint it Black
Clinton's toasting Yeltsin:
    "Zdrovye Bourgeois Flack!"

[& Yeltsin replies (spoken):
"YUPTVOYOMAT! (go fuck your mother)
murderer, sex maniac!"]

I spoke to Tolstoy: "Emma
    Goldman's coming back!"
He sat there writing on a
    shard of red & black
Black & Red. Coming back!
Red & Black. They're comin'
    back!

The Homeless Alien morphs to
    Newt's Sonovabitch
The Species [Social] Being's
    served up: dessert for the
    rich
The Lions of Reason strobe
    the deep grave of yr dream

The Lamb of Love hides in the
    Caves of Academe.

I hear the students as they
    wonder what comes next
They're forced to take the test
    but do not have the text
They wander thru the World
    Wild Internet
They still believe they'll find
    the Finland Station yet! [in
    St. Petersburg where
    Lenin and other exiled radicals
    entered Russia in 1917]

I heard Mohr [Marx] & The
    General [Engels] laughing
    in their Hell
They said Bakunyin had a fun-
    ny tale to tell:
"Anarcho Pacifist Bolshevism never
    had its chance!"
Perhaps we cd invite St. Fran-
    cis to the dance? And hey
    St. Paul & Jacob Frank!
    [18cent PolJewCath pan-
    sexualist Messiah]
    YOWZAH!

I see The White House & I
    want to paint it Red
Willy Reich is shouting at me:
    "Better Bed than Dead!"
Now Billy's roasting Yeltsin:
    "So long Klatura Hack!"
I spy The Kremlin Hey we're
    gonna take it back!

RED & BLACK
GET IT BACK
RED & BLACK
WE'RE COMIN' BACK
RED & BLACK
RED & BLACK
RED & BLACK

TULI KUPFERBERG

Sharon Mesmer

Bad Day on Avenue A
a rant for Pat Buchanan

I dreamt I woke up naked in Katz's and said to Pat Buchanan
eating a corned beef sandwich, "In terms of art and culture,
just mind your own business, be a good pedestrian, make
only sweeping generalizations, as private references make
any good time decrepit. Can I offer you a hogwash cock-
tail? A tour of the underclass? Life may be expensive but at
least *you* can get another beer, to drown your politically
savvy sadness. I can't be an authority on everything and
still be a poet, because, as far as poetry goes, the dumber I
am the better. I'm sure you've noticed by now that there's
nothing at stake in my personality, but I know that the vio-
lence we see in movies is really just the instinctively feared
'otherness' of homosexuals, black people, girls, perfor-
mance artists, the homeless and the unemployed,
subtextualized and made available for middle-class tastes.
Personally I'm just slumming my way through this cul-
ture, dispassionately picking up metaphors like an anteater,
waking up every morning and wondering, 'Is this East Ber-
lin, circa August 13, 1961 yet?' I refrain from calling my
predicament a 'lifestyle choice,' because after all I am just
a delicatessen intellectual, hustling for dates down Broad-
way with a clipboard, thinking of someone I love dancing
romantically with someone I hate, the violins like mosqui-
toes whining on and on at the Psychotic Ballroom, the per-
vasive and familiar springtime armpit smell… But I'm
secure in the knowledge that what I feel in my cheap room
is not felt by Exxon's millionaires in their comfortable
homes, and that it's a good feeling to fuck and live to tell
about it, Pat, n'est-ce-pas?"

Daniel Moore

From "A Visit to the Graves of the Bosnian Muslims"

I went to the open graves of Bosnian Muslim victims of
    genocide
and leaned down into gaping holes like mouth of
    Jonah's whale and saw
bloodied bodies massed together,
old men with tears in their beards and old women,
scarves embroidered with blood-red roses tight around
    chins,
young women with babies still at their breast,
young men with faces of angels like full moons with
    slit throats
        bleeding light,
and I asked them about their state,

and they all opened their eyes and said: *We're in Paradise.*
We walk through green gardens and sit by sweet fountains,
we drink from rivers of milk and honey, we fly in the
beaks of green birds, we sit with the
    Prophet Muhammad, God's peace be upon him,
and gaze on his face of gentle purity and he gazes back at us,
God asks us to enter His Garden,
we bathe in the Light of His Face
and are at peace—

...and the young men with faces of angels opened their eyes
and said: *Here in Paradise we've won!*
We don't need to watch anymore as our world blows apart,
    we were alone in the world
        but here we have company,
yet we feel sorry for the people on earth who
never helped us or even helped us defend ourselves,

we fear Hell's flames will lick their bodies like
     bloodthirsty beasts and
consume them,
their faces will be shocked
and they'll wonder why such brutal heartbreak is
     happening to them
just as we wondered
     why it was happening to us,
why our own neighbors killed us with
     shovels and kitchen knives and raped our mothers
          and sisters,
just for the crime of wanting to live together
in peace—

…and the middle-aged fathers opened their eyes, and said:
They shot us down from high mountaintops, they
squeezed us into
trucks and took us to death camps
and the world was silent, day after day
the world was silent as stone,
they starved us to death while
well-dressed people with new haircuts sat in
air-conditioned palaces and
discussed the "Bosnian situation"
plump politicians worried about re-election
discussed the "Bosnian situation" day after day
while we held out our hands to them
their hearts encased in blocks of ice,
…they watched as professors, scientists, poets,
     farmers and merchants
became homeless skeletal men and women
scrounging in refugee camps
forced to eat shoe leather—

And the young women and mothers opened their eyes,
     and said:
What happened to us was unspeakable—

…then they cleared their throats and said:

Perhaps the Secretary-General was too busy to notice us,
perhaps there was another war more important than
    ours,
perhaps they finally dropped some bombs on the
    enemies of decency,
perhaps some of our country was returned to us,
but our mosques were destroyed
and the hearts of our children were soured,
our past was turned to dust and our future
    to rust...

they all closed their eyes again, the mothers and
fathers, grandmothers and grandfathers, young men and
women, and the babies,
and I heard them all whisper:

The earthly doors have closed and we no longer hear
    human voices,
we eat sweet fruits and drink sweet nectar pouring from
    rocks,
we live in cool atmospheres and look on the
    faces of our loved ones,
        and the blood has been wiped away...
we ask God to take the terror from the hearts of our enemies
just as the terror has gone from our hearts here in
    Paradise.

We have no more fear here in Paradise.

We have no more worries here in God's Garden.

Eileen Myles

From "Mr. Twenty"

Won't somebody stop
this man. The first thing we learned
was the world would end
in our time. Do you think
we give a shit by now
Lying at the bottom of the
toilet of the naked
emperor, every time
he flushes we're supposed
to applaud. We do not.
We yawn. That was a
really big turd the emperor
just made. Must be
for women we giggled.
Huh. I lifted my
glass to my lips
it's mostly silence now
the regular darkening
as he puts his fanny
down on the lid of the
century. It makes me just
want to do something great
for the world. If there's
another big race riot in
America I think I'll go
direct streetcar named
desire in the midst of
it. I'm sick of doing nothing
I want to help.
Naturally I'll play Stanley
an angry white lesbian
walking through the burning

streets yelling Stella
Yeah. I'm eager. I'm rubbing
my palms. No seriously
folks I was born
just a few years after the
Emperor put some big bombs
down. It was very
fertile ground. I remember
a screaming sound in the
sky but the world seemed silent
that day & then some
ashes fell, or maybe it
was a scrap of worn out
rubber from the side
of the road
somehow it fell from
the sky.

Carl Rakosi

DOWN TO EARTH SUITE

I

Museum of Historical Objects
    New Acquisition

an honest word
(embalmed in amber)
out of Washington

as rare
as hippopotamus meat

or a blade of timothy
behind a bumpkin's ear.

II

The Realists

Let us be honest,
there are the poor,

the virtuous, the artists
weeping at injustice,

and there are the realists
who secretly admire the rich

and cultivate rapacity,
who are always well-bred

and decently non-commital
like the upper classes

but implacable
in their self-interest.

III

The Common People

The boys down at the local bar
drinking to the companionship
of men had their own ideas about this
but waited for their senior sage,
Mr. Dooley, to expound it. After
a decent interval and a boilermaker,
Mr. Dooley cleared his throat
and began: "The American nation
in the Sixth Ward is a fine people"
… the men's ears perked up and
they started to chuckle, waiting
for the punch line… Mr. Dooley
continued… "they love the eagle
on the back of a dollar."

IV

The Reality

How are you?

Why do you ask?
Not floating
like a sea turtle

in chelonian
bliss,
I can tell you.

And you?

Can't say.
Too busy.

We're looking
for the right axis.

And you? What
are you feeling?

the state
of the world
… flaky…

a ship passing
in the night,
calling:

Idealists aboard!
we're quarantined
we can't land.

V

Idea

the ultimate
        poem;
God sat
        on His throne
and shat!

Nanao Sakaki

In Honor of the Persian Gulf War

Before robbery
There was ownership.

Before ownership
There were things

Before things
There was nothing.

Before nothing
There was robbery.

Janine Pommy Vega

The Draft

Walking out or into a prison for the fiftieth or hundredth
    time
to encounter by chance a "draft,"
the bringing in of prisoners to their new abode,
to watch the men shuffle in in shackles
ankles in chains wrists in chains
ordinary men, their dignity crumpled about
their feet like regulation greens on the floor
of the crapper, where do you put your eyes?

How, like Pablo Neruda, who came holding out
his hands in front of him, filthy from the blood
of the mines, can you take no part in the crime?
Called "on the draft," a routine procedure,
as though naming it would efface the squalor
a euphemism like "on the way to the showers"
at Auschwitz, "she's on relief detail for the troops,"
how do you witness? Where do you put your eyes?

In World War I, World War II
men drafted to defend their country
are pulled in now to bolster an industry
building on their shackles at the bottom of the pile
two million strong. Lamp shades, anyone?
And to see it weekly, regularly, to come upon it
fresh at the gate, or the central cage,

or the bench on the guardroom floor,
do you engage the man who does not want
to be seen with rage in your eyes? With compassion?
Do you look somewhere else in the drab
environment for relief? Do you ignore

the chains the civilization you belong to
put on his hands, his feet? Do you bow your head
in shame? Do you ask for forgiveness?

Careful no trace of it reaches your face, you
double over with the sucker punch
you are on your hands and knees in the sewer
plowing through defilement
Uniformed men corraling raw material into clumps
are workers in the world, like you
engaged in the transport of people in chains
as a day job, how does that feel?

If this were an isolated instance
you could tell the story to a shocked world
rocked in its innate decency to demand redress
but it is common

The cruelty has grown from random acts
to a root cause the size of a grapefruit
a tumor in the heart of a people
and try as you will there is no way to avoid it
or engage in gallows humor and forget it,
there is nowhere you can turn and not see it,
the guilt of complicity falls on the shoulders
of all who will not speak, who avert our eyes.

BORN AGAIN BLUES

Orphaned orphaned Mommy & Daddy done gone
(again)
I've got that inner traumatized American white child
　　within wanna wail all night long

She's got a wrinked hag's body itching and bitching
　　inside
(again)
She's gonna come out raging & demonize the countryside

Born again born again let those fundamentalist inner
　　child demons pollute the sky
(again)
I'm gonna burn all you pro-choice queer atheists just to
　　see you fry

Life's no fun unless you're fighting the lord god's holy war
(again)
He's got a mean eye-for-an-eye-doctrine— it says you
　　burn in the Bible— save you from from Satan's door

Amendment 2s Measure 9s all around the USA
(again)
See the laws change, get on the school boards give
　　creationists, bigots, racists the right o' way

O I'm born again born again you got see it my
  escatological way
(again)
I've got a right to sing the blues too get everyone on their
  knees n' pray

But in the dark of the night I just can't find any peace
Out on the street by day I'm haunted by this born again
  fundamentalist disease
So consumed hating phantom enemy can't find any
  release

Born again born again shriek it to the skies
(again)
Got that born again inner demon child inside telling me
  crazy lies.

Peter Lamborn Wilson

The Sacred and Profane History of Money

The first coin was not a practical means of symbolizing exchange (as the economists believe): — the earliest coins were temple tokens, pilgrimage souvenirs, detachable bits of holy power, made of substances at once chthonic (underground) & celestial (sun/moon, gold/silver) — an exchange not between humans but between humans & spirits.

As coinage is "secularized" it already appears as debased & polluted with lesser metals, subject to "inflation." But *inflation* is breath, i.e. spirit. Money begins as half spirit half material, a doorway between worlds. But money becomes ever more spiritualized as it circulates through "History." Money is a *gnostic system*, or an *imaginal machine*. "Advances" in the abstraction of exchange are often introduced by mystical orders, as for example the perfection of chequing-systems by the Assassins & Templars. Banking appears as a kind of alchemy, making wealth out of credit, something out of nothing. And the whole process can be summed up by the U.S. dollar bill, a virtual crypto-text on the occult nature of money.

The Hermetic philosophers of the Renaissance revealed the secrets of money, but their theories were debunked as mumbo-jumbo — and secretly appropriated by the masters of a new paradigm whereby money was launched completely into the world of pure spirit (or "rational mind," its secular shadow).

Etherialized as sheer representation, money could become paper (text) backed by metal, then by imaginary metal, then by sheer imagination — pure textuality. By the 18th century all nation-states were in debt to their own self-created banks. By 1973 the long alchemical process ended with Nixon's "toppling the gold standard," a feat of pure heraldic magic.

The "Global Market" manifests as a gnostic sphere in which thought, transmitted at digital speed, coagulates as symbolic wealth. By now two trillion dollars a day whirl around the globe in a noosphere (or "numisphere") of their own, devouring all such lesser ideologies as communism or democracy. "Money's gone to Heaven," become absolutely pure, & all-powerful. *This* is the future. *This* is the Millennium.

Allen Ginsberg

New Democracy Wish List
for President Clinton White House

Retro Axioms:

"Progress" ended in XX century.

Hyper-rationalism reduces natural complexity of nature
through narrow thought abstraction; Hyper-
rationalization, hyper-industrialization & Hyper-
technology create chaos.

U.S. command economy subsidizes fossil fuel and
nuclear Energy & Science, Agriculture, Air &
Motor Transport, Banking, Communications,
Military Industrial Complex, licit & illicit psycho-
active Drugs, also rules Mass Media via FCC.
American Free Market is hi-tech myth with
national socialist centralized regulation implicit
everywhere except small business & little maga-
zines.

Muscle power connected to appropriate hi-tech might
rehabilitate Earth.

Lacks & Needs:

Fossil Fuels retard the planet. Detoxify America: tainted
Fire poisons Earth, fouls Air & pollutes Water.

Emphasize prevention & alternative medicine with
medical insurance rebates for not using Self-
insured health credits: like mythic China, "Only
pay Doctor when you are well."

Fund Ryan White Care Act, separate Church & State in
    Center for Disease Control, fund bleach kits,
    needle exchange & plainspoken AIDS education,
    build infrastructure of decentralized community
    based health care preventative medicine early
    intervention clinics for poverty class disease-prone
    high-risk teens women & men living with AIDS &
    TB inner city plagues.

Coordinate National crash program to research inexpen-
    sive anti-AIDS medicines.

Separate Church & State in arts, education & civil law.
    Restore National Endowment for the Arts & FCC
    freedom from Fundamentalist political intrusion.

Sexuality's loose not fixed. Legalize it.

Decriminalize addictive drug problem, doctors can cure
    addiction or provide maintenance if no cure.
    Reduce mass-million expense on narcotics-
    addicted political prisoners overcrowding courts &
    jails, Medicalize drug trade.

Decriminalize marijuana, its disadvantages are minor;
    reserve hemp grass as unadvertised private small
    cash crop for failing family farms, encourage
    hemp fabric industries.

Privatize & entrust psychedelics to medical educational
    priestly professions. End Military monopoly on
    LSD research and development.

End tobacco farming subsidies, cut use. Ex-Nicotine
    lobbyists working in Clinton's new White House
    can stop smoking.

Shift agricultural subsidies toward grain beans &
   vegetable diet. Tax meat as a nutritional agronomic
   & ecologic disaster.

With massive scale reforestation rural & in wilderness,
   plant also universal urban tree rows.

Establish Civilian Conservation Corps for Urban home-
   steading, thin out corrupt local bureaucracies
   obstructing populist housing reconstruction.

Encourage international trade in Eco-technology in place
   of enabling codependency on weapons trade.

Inaugurate National "Limits of Growth" Program for
   Population/Land Use/Pollution.

Jump start national state & city human and industrial
   waste compost & recycling.

Honor primary and secondary school teachers, elevate
   respect, reward educators as handsomely as
   Plumbers, reduce class crowding to human size,
   under 15 students; encourage national child-care
   projects.

Take back money from SLA bankruptcy profiteer goniffs.

Purge U.S. military death squad subsidies in Salvador,
   Guatemala, etc. We backed up dictators in Zaire,
   Somalia, Liberia, Sudan, Angola, Haiti, Iran, Iraq,
   Salvador, we're responsible: admit it then figure
   ways out.

Open CIA & FBI & NSA archives on Cointelpro raids,
   Government drug dealing, Kennedy/King assassi-

nations, Iranian Contragate, Panama Deception,
Vatican, Hand & Lavoro Bank thuggery, etc.
including Bush-Noriega relations and other CIA
client-agent scandals.

Open all secret files on J. Edgar Hoover-Cardinal
Spellman-Roy Cohn-Joe McCarthy alcoholic
Closet-Queen Conspiracy with Organized Crime
to sabotage the U.S. Labor Movement, Native
African-American Hispanic & Gay minority
leaderships; and blackmail U.S. Presidents
Congress each other for half century.

Get Government Secret Police (DEA CIA FBI NSA etc.)
off our backs by the next millennium.

January 17, 1993

II. Allen Ginsberg as Poet-Activist

Allen Ginsberg

TELEVISION ADDRESS
[1972 REPUBLICAN NATIONAL CONVENTION]

My name: Allen Ginsberg, responding to this station's editorial denouncing violent behavior of some protesters at Republican Convention proceedings at Miami Beach late August (1972).

A small minority, anti-war movement protesters, fringe-group of hysterical kids, attacked cars and buses carrying North Carolina's Nixon Republicans to Miami's convention hall. Some few delegates were directly struck. The war-protest majority sanely sat on streets Ghandi-style, non-violent, offering their bodies for arrest. Half-dozen pacifist organizers fasted a month. There were sit ins, speeches, street theater, and marches; an elephant dragged a black coffin to the convention hall.

Did any of you see Dave Dellinger's starved saintly face and sensible voice on television? You saw kids trashing instead, right? Dellinger fasted for forty days through Miami to protest Republican Indochina war violence, the greatest single episode of man-made violence ever wreaked on earth! Did you hear bony faced Dellinger remind us of the four million tons of bombs (twice the weight of all bombs dropped in W.W. II) dropped on Indochina in Nixon's last 3 1/2 years?

The righteous Nixon Republican conventioneers didn't renounce a 4 year old policy of guava bomblets and vomit gas! Propane incendiary super bombs! Dragontooth plastic pellet gravel mines! Flechette barbed-nail cluster bombs! Napalm-phosphorous-thermite anti-human splashbombs! Project Igloo White the automated electronic computerized air battlefield that's already murdered half a million people! Mostly innocent peasants in ricefields, 80% of Vietnam's bombs were dropt on South Vietnam! Over a million injured! More than five million homeless refugees from U.S.A. bombing in Nixon's 3 1/2 years!

Did the proud Nixon North Carolina delegates know these facts? Did they care? Wasn't it our own official government violence that washed half-way round the world and touched us with a wavelet of horror?

I was teargassed sitting on the street praying AH! A few police-infiltrated peace protesters spoiled the scene for many more sane anti-war fold. But what of the bland double-think of the North Carolina delegates who came accepting Nixon's "handling of the war" including 4 million tons of bombs. This is science-fiction style, dehumanized, remote control mass violence.

—Allen Ginsberg speaking extemporaneously in Charlotte, NC, 1972, previously unpublished

Eugene Brooks

Poem for Allen Ginsberg

Wherever you hover, Spirit, mind-deep in space
Where God signs his name in hydrogen italics
Among Oort cloud comets that brought water to Earth
For our throats' thirsts and tears for our eyes;
Or drifting over mountain crags west of Boulder
Where you touch ethereal fingers to wingtips of eagles;
Or under the world's oceans admonishing sharks
To clamp their teeth into little fish more thoughtfully;
Or lounging among Cherry Valley ferns, watching with
    daisies' eyes
Through a lattice of tree twigs a red sun sliver
Slide below the horizon's rim; nightfall crickets chirp
The compact epics of their lives; or sitting with us
Invisible in the 13th Street Fifth floor eyrie
As church bells toll the heartbeat of time into song,
Now you know all, Allen, while earthbound our senses
    fail.
You can see time gone and time to come, how the
    Cosmos started and ends,
How the rose builds its lovely carbon body out of
    photons and rain.
You watch the girl in her bedroom cursing the face in the
    mirror,
You watch the long legged stripling toss
Basketballs through hoops— move on, you're past all sex.

Well, hardline Capitalism triumphed in your time,
It had to, crushing your outcries in a torrent of plastic,
Toyotas, color TV, computers, digital disks;
The doe-eyed, the misfits still cram jails and bughouses,
The Statue of David shines in the Academy
While Europe and Africa pile up their corpse mountains.

61

So shower your pity on the nation you scolded;
Pity our soldier dragged in Mogadishu dust,
Pity the homeless in their cardboard chapels,
Pity the neck-slashed girl and the death cell halfwit,
Pity our midnight soul fears and dark dream tremors;
Pity our workplace gouging of each other
That our children not fall under the spiked wheel of
        poverty,
Pity the comrades you wordlessly deserted,
Pity your brother's self-pity, the vanity of his grief.
Pity the human race its illusion of permanence.

Eileen Myles

A Speech about Allen

Allen was more of a star than a homosexual. His great triumph was that you forgot he was gay. He was so many things that produced that one thing which was Allen Ginsberg, again and again and so when you try and see him as gay, you still only see him as Allen. One thing I can say about being queer in America today is that for instance if you are already famous you can say you are gay and quickly that becomes all that people see. On the other hand you could be famous and everybody knows you are gay and you never say it, and people watch you in the public sector and it's like the silent partner, your homosexuality and everyone watches you and wonders when you will stand up for them, why won't she come out, but they also admire you for being famous and forgive you for wanting to stay there, all glossy and bright and understand that you don't want to lose your seat on that wonderful promontory of fame for being queer. Allen was nearly thrown out of Russia for being queer, and I think part of his pleasure in being famous was adding that one thing in all the time, so that if they forgot Allen Ginsberg was queer, which was easy because he was so many things, then he would remind them that he liked to suck boys cocks and the honor that was bestowed on him, the acceptance, would be nearly taken away, and the *nearly* is really important, I don't know the story up close, I just remember the incident and the boat of State shaking, light and full of drama, shaking really hard like something was going to happen, Allen provoked that by saying who he was, and then it was *just true* and the boat arighted itself. Allen knew how to stay with it. He "put his queer shoulder to the wheel."

I think about being gay in America right now and how for instance for a moment our president stood up for us, briefly, he tried to make it okay for gays in the military, and everyone knows the military is loaded with queers, is it only gay people who know that any same sex organization is intrinsically more gay than straight, girls' schools, camps, scouts, gym, and all these conventional places where the culture celebrates wholesomeness and youth, gay people just laugh and remember sneaking around and lusting and fearing exposure and craving it in some way, exposure. Almost being caught is hot. So keep that in mind, the exciting fear of exposure, playing it close, and think of the famous American poet Allen Ginsberg who loved to sing about losing his cherry to HP in Provincetown, naked Allen, who lived by exposure.

So the way things wound up in the military is that the ship of state started rocking again, and, see, the problem is, our president isn't gay. He couldn't stay out there. He had to back down. The solution in the military was that you can do anything you want, you just can't talk about it, and no one can ask you either, and the responsibility for homosexuality is put back on the queer in a very strange way, as if the compulsion to tell were the irresistible part of being gay, as if coming out was the thing that has to stop, and no one *really* minds women fucking women and men fucking men, and if we would just do it quietly like heterosexuals do, then everything would be okay.

And then you turn on the teevee and there's a cute romance, and then you change the channel and there's a show about a young girl coming of age and liking a boy, and then you watch another show about Seinfeld having a naked woman cleaning his apartment, and it's really funny and of course you're bombarded with images of heterosexuality all day long, the man in the deli flirts with me, he just assumes I'm straight, and all the women in the clothes catalogues are eventually in a canoe with a man, if you're successful eventually you have to find a mate, it's just part of being human, to not stand alone, to put one person next to the other one, and everybody applauds. But what if we stopped that, if we suggested for a moment that, yes, it is okay to silently mate and breed, and come of age and think about the opposite sex, but no school dances please and no proms, and no weddings, and no cute blind date plots on teevee, no rock n roll, no movies about love, and no Valentines Day, and no in-laws, and no tax breaks, no celebrations of what you do, no songs, and no schools for your kids because we don't know how *that* happened, why should we pay for it, and no health insurance for more than one person in your house because then we'll have to think about what you do, and the fact that we are essentially paying for you living together and doing it all the time, is really disturbing, as if we should take care of that, your "love" as you call it, your lifestyle, two lousy bodies lying in bed in a house for years and the offspring of your shame, kids three and four of them, hundreds and thousand of them across America, forcing everyone to think repeatedly about you copulating in your beds at night for years, the loud bed creaking, a culture built around the repetition of that love, and Allen Ginsberg kept insisting that he was your baby. He stood there singing, beautiful and goofy with his little suitcase, at the door of the ship of state, for forty years, and he said that he was home.

— Speech originally delivered at Planet News, a tribute to Allen Ginsberg's poetry and social activism, Cathedral of St. John the Divine, New York City, 5/14/98.

Edward Sanders

Remarks Written for the Dedication of a Dogwood Tree in Honor of Allen Ginsberg in the Poets Grove at St. Mark's Church April 18, 1999

He was a great bard
He was a great friend
He was a great American
He made it his business
to know the intricacies of his nation
more so than any other
          bard in our history

He did his
     high-metabolism best
to be a part of the history
               of his time.
Once he called
Henry Kissinger
when Kissinger was Secretary of State
& got through to him
     —he wanted Kissinger to meet with Dave Dellinger
     on ending the war in Vietnam.

His legacy
     is a service to freedom,
tolerance and the spreading
of the power of poetry
for human good.

For over 40 years
he wrote great poetry
     that throbbed its way into
          the world wide culture

No other bard ever
traveled so much
     as Irwin Allen Ginsberg
son of a Communist mother
& a Social Democrat dad
who went to Columbia U
        hoping to become a labor attorney

He made his poetry
part of the culture of Europe, India, China,
Japan, & Eastern Europe

He had at least 10,000 friends
most of whom no doubt
     felt his bardic grace
       & bacchic energy
         passing through their lives.

He brought wild curiosity
     into poetry
—Have you ever known a poet
     to ask so many questions
       in his poetry?
He also brought a wild eroticism into poetry
in a way not seen since
     Catullus

He took on the excesses of the
Military-Industrial Complex
in a multi-decade campaign
unmatched by any
     other bard
       in world history

No other bard ever
did so many benefits
or raised so much money

to help his friends.

He set up a bardic system
like no other Poet I think
I call it the Forest Ginsberg.

No other bard in world history
had a 25 pages
press contact list
        for instance

He was probably the greatest
workaholic
        in the history of world poetry
I was talking w/ Raymond Foye
            a few days ago
and I had to chuckle
when Raymond
remarked how it would take Allen
15 minutes to describe all
the projects for which he was currently
                on deadline

He was a workaholic to the end—
They were about to
bring in recording equipment
to do his MTV special
from his sick bed
        when time ran out.

And so I salute
a hundred times
        & then a 1,000 times
a great American bard
Allen Ginsberg

Amiri Baraka

To Allen: Hail & Farewell

HOWL reached Puerto Rico, late 55, whenever the early Village Voice did. I was there disguised as a colored Airman second-class, lower left gunner and weather man on a B36, Reading at nights and 12 hrs every day under the Latino sun, while guarding somebody else's airplanes, and scoffing every stationery word in English Literature, all the Best sellers in the NY Times and with 7 or so comrades in an underground airman professional killer salon learning the history of western music and literature as night librarian at Ramey Air Force Base, Strategic Air Command, Aquadilla Puerto Rico. At least two of those guys, both photographers, lurk somewhere even now in NYC, to tell the tale. James Lucas and Phil Perkis!

We read and kicked Hardy, Proust, Kafka. Hey, What's a Kafka, we yelled?. I donno...Hey Roi order it. And the night librarian did, plus a fifth of Rum. Motets, Gregorian Chants, Bach, Ulysses, Tess Durburville, I mean some under the earth dull as shit, but Ulysses, Rimbaud, Baudelaire, Satie. We were getting our under over graduate readiness preparation to return to Civilization, we thought, after roaming the sky scaring the world with nuclear frustration, American ignorance and young arrogance, wandering what the big world wd be.

For me, the Voice, was just more confirmation that like my High School hero Allen Polite, who I first was turned on to The Writer, him a still great unpublished Poet. HE said, we thought, The VILLAGE, YEH, thats where everything was at! OH yeh. Thats where the world class intellectuals and knowers wd reside. Oh Yeh.

And finally, 1957, they booted me out as undesirable, you bet, I had already got booted out of College as likewise, but now as a fucking commie buddhist colored guy, busted for books and an alarming hostility to dumbness. You ever dig Curtis Lemay on his stomach on a go cart speeding across the flight line Saturday mornings. Wd instruct the hell out of you. With both stripes now ripped off along with secret clearance, Gone Gone, and so we shot off in ecstasy to the City the Apple, New York, Bohemia, The Village, to try out our vicious learning on those we were sure wd dig how heavy we had got.

And it was Howl again. Plus Allan Polite and his cohorts, Cunningham, Cage, Charlip, Czernovitch, RhBlythe, Suzuki, Zen, gals in black stockings, Yeats, Poetry Poetry Poetry, that brought us panting into the Village. 1st crib 104 E.3d St, 28S a month 3 rms no heat, my mother wept. But hey wasn't this the joint?

But Alas! and Alas and Alack. IT was not that what that was in my head. Not the GV of PR. The west village was full of poseurs and empty bags of old pretense where was Poetry. Where was heavy intellectual outness after all? But Howl was emerging full then. Being talked about Given Ink emerging full and clear. What struck me…an Audaciousness I needed….in that McCarthy Eisenhower 7 Types of Ambiguity 50's. That oatmeal lying world. In Puerto Rico, I'd sent my stuff to Kenyon, Sewanee, Hudson, Partisan, and all the cemeteries, and it came back almost before being mailed. The New Yorker's poetry actually made me weep, at the deep nothingness they touted as feeling, yeh, but only of deep disgust.

So HOWL— the language. The stance. The sense of someone being in the same world, the defiance. Yeh— to the Dead and somebody else's version of a Bohemian Intelligentsia there was here this HOWL. So I wrote Allen on a piece of toilet paper to Git Le Couer asking was he for real. He answered on french toilet paper, which is better for writing, that he was tired of being Allen

Ginsberg. And sent a broad registration of poetry for the new magazine YUGEN. And that began some forty years of hookup.

Allen was finally what I thought was everywhere in the Village, a genuine book stuffed intellectual, and as well, a publicist, perhaps the best we knew of poetry itself. There were so many bullshitters and tasters and energetic dilettantes otherwise. Jammed in the coffee shops imitating Marlon Brando. Except Jack Micheline wasnt imitating, in those jazz poetry sessions he was who Marlon Brando was imitating.

And we remained friends Allen and I for 40 years. His takes on Williams, and the variable foot, American speech, the breath phrase, the existence of an American language and literature, which the colleges still deny, was what was most important to me. The anti Moloch heavy anti imperialist line that wove through HOWL. AMERICA Go FUCK YR SELF WITH YR ATOM BOMB! Now that was poetry! Plus talking to Allen bout Western poetry was always part of a course. On Blake, Smart, Rimbaud, the troubadours, we visited Pound and he apologized for being anti Semitic at least Allen heard that, that crazzy motherfucker. Wms funeral, we trooped over for, Weequahic high school, in Newark where we was both borned. Howard U, that historic trek, reading on the campus, refused from all buildings.

Allen was a font of ideas and publicity for the new word, a new generation, on prosody, America and intros to the whole united front against dead people "they dont like the way we live" was the way AG summed it up. And for this, that we cd bring the SFS, the Beats, the Black Mt., OHara and the NYErs together to do battle against the zombies of Euroformalism, neo colonial death verse was where our deepest comradeship was formed.

Allen and I argued relentlessly, soon as he and me, we went our separate ideological practical day to day paths. Malcolms murder shot me out of the village for good, and our greetings and meeting became measure less frequent. The gap between Black nationalism and Tibetan Buddhism, I wanted to make War, Allen to make peace. For all our endless contention, often loud and accompanied by contrasting histrionics we remained, in many ways, comrades in and of the word, partisans of consciousness!

The day before he split Allen called and sd he had to see me. Very important he sd. Can you come. Yeh, whats up. Well...he paused, then as usual, matter of fact— I'm gonna die... OH bullshit, Allen Whyre you saying that? No— It's true. I just got out the hospital. Maybe a couple months...not long. Hey dont say dumb shit like that. No No its true...Anyway you need any money? Money? Naw Naw I dont need no money ...and you aint gonna die. Well, you still gonna come Monday, its important. Yeh, I'll be there....but nix on that death shit. Ok, see you...we exchanged our outs...the phone hit. Then the next day, the newspapers carried their stuff. A big drag...Man, a big big drag, you know. Because that fundamental struggle for American poetry. For our speech and consciousness as part of the energy and power of the United front against the dead and their Ghosts. The anti imperialist revolutionary democratic struggle itself is still running again at Rage Pt.

But then a last word for Allen, gone now, turned completely into spirit on us. What we uphold, is the defiance and resistance to Moloch, in the collective tongue of the multinational multi cultural American tongue and voice. What it was I first dug he was saying in Howl. And the great line from America. America go fuck yr self with yr Atom Bomb. Now that's Poetry!! That still rings and will ring true. And for this sentiment, and stance, and revolutionary democratic practice, part of revolutionary art for cultural revolution, we say Hail and Farewell my man, Hail and Farewell